Because I Am More Than JUST My Skin

Motivated By: Mikkita L Moore

Because I Am More Than JUST My Skin

Because I Am More Than JUST My Skin

ISBN: 978-1-7354792-2-4
Imprint: Invisible Daughter, LLC
Printed and bounded in the United States of America.

Because I Am More Than JUST My Skin

Because I Am More Than JUST My Skin

<u>THANK YOU!!!</u>

Because I Am More Than JUST My Skin

Special Thanks & Dedication

Thank all of you for making this book possible

All the Authors: *Mikkita L Moore, Nina Thomas (Nina Motivates), Latonya Willett, KeiSha Osgood, Alicia Hall, Conchetta Jones, Q.R. Williams- Oaks*

Graphic Designer: *Shawn Robinson, of 727 Marketing... It's been a pleasure to work with you!!*

This book is dedicated to all the girls that had and have to "BECOME" comfortable in their own skin. For all the girls that had to learn to love themselves no matter what! This one is for you!

Table of Content

Because I Am More Than JUST My Skin

Chapter One

Black Gal

Mikkita L. Moore

Mikkita L Moore, an author, motivational speaker and mother of five, starting at the tender age of 14 from the South Side of Chicago. Mikkita is a retired, master stylist and cosmetology instructor. She has owned two successful hair salons over a period of 13 years and an event-planning company, *Symply Plyzurez Eventz* since 2004. Mikkita is the Founder and CEO of *The Art of Transparency, NFP* an organization with a mission to "Heal ONE Person, One City, ONE State, ONE Nation at a time". The CEO of *Invisible Daughter, LLC* a publishing and Writing Coach Company. Although passionate about teaching others about her journey which includes forgiving a father that wasn't, in her opinion, able to be the model man she had desperately needed as a young girl growing into womanhood, she continued to struggle with her inner feelings. Being able to convey these imbedded emotions is also comforting for her. Learning the *Art of Transparency* is equivalent to facing and being fully aware of who she is, her ability to candidly speak from the heart about real life issues and how to conquer life's trials is one of my greatest gifts.

Speaking to participants is a time for meaningful engagement. Time used to encourage, lead and offer real life situations and results to enable listeners to truly understand and connect with her, not only as the speaker but to have empathy for the topic. One of the results that Mikkita obtains when speaking to audiences is her dynamic ability to ignite an awakening within those who hear her story. It allows them to realize and understand their issue more clearly, that she has been through similar situations and how they, too, can overcome the feelings and possible stagnations from its impact. These processes are all facilitated with audience in mind.

How beneficial it is to have the skill to ignite the path of change. Mikkita's niche is engaging her teen pregnancy and parenting audiences with realistic topics that help identify the issues and the teens' willingness to work towards resolutions. Her books, *The Letter From, the Invisible Daughter* as well as *The Cause and Effect of The Invisible Daughter*, talks about, among other topics, parenting a child that's different from the rest and her doubts of being a good mother. As she speaks candidly about her thoughts of suicide and being in unsafe relationships that included domestic violence; emotional, mental and physical, she creates and implements strategies to be used in the moment to begin healing processes for others. Most gatherings include hands-on activities. There's only room for results; a growth mindset. Mikkita continues to receive multiple invites to speak due this direct approach which call for peace and progress in the lives of others.

During the pandemic of 2020, Mikkita was blessed to birth another five books through collaborations with other Authors. By the end of 2020, Mikkita will have Authored a total of ten books collectively. With all of my books I wanted to reach my audience on a level that's different from the rest. I needed to reach an audience that hasn't heard about the Black girl from the south side of Chicago that wasn't poor and not knowing where her next meal would come from. The girl that her mother wasn't a drug addict, father wasn't a drug pusher. I was tired of the stereo types that I had to be from this type of family or that kind of family because I had my first child at the age of 14 years old. My all-time favorite was the one that says teenage moms can't raise their children effectively or the one that says teenage moms are all high school drop outs. Neither of which proves true for me.

My books are not about the average poor Black girl living in poverty. My book is about my life, from a perspective of a teenage mom that didn't struggle, that didn't drop out of high school but in fact graduated high school a year ahead of time with honors. This book is my life from a perspective that thought about suicide, went through domestic violence, emotionally mentally and physically. This book talks from a perspective of not feeling the love of my father searching for that type of love from boys/men that either couldn't give it or just didn't know how to give love.

My books talk about parenting a child that's different from the rest of her five children. Wondering where I went wrong as a parent, or as a real mother. I talk about being fatherless and how that affects my relationships with men. In my books I talk about how my struggle with alcohol was the only way I could cope with the depression and anger that was built from all the "life issues" that I didn't know how to let go of. My books come from real life situations that happens in our community far too often and over looked because it's not society's "norm".

Mikkita along with her tour has scheduled and appeared for several presentations and speaking engagements, over the last 4 years with heightened interest in each state. Moving forward there will be plans to host back-to-school events, expos, workshops and conferences on healing awareness.

Mikkita L Moore

www.mikkitamoore.com

info@mikkitamoore.com

Black Gal

The Bible says.....

Ephesians 2:10 ESV
For we are his workmanship, created in Christ Jesus for good works, which God prepared beforehand, that we should walk in them.

Genesis 1:27 ESV
So God created man in his own image, in the image of God he created him; male and female he created them.

Psalm 139:14 ESV
I praise you, for I am fearfully and wonderfully made. Wonderful are your works; my soul knows it very well.

However for me.....

I remember being about 4 years old sitting in the kitchen getting my hair pressed and curled for Easter Sunday. When my mama gave me the mirror to look at my hair, I immediately smiled and said that I was the pretty princess. I loved getting my hair combed as a young girl. Living in the home with my mama (really my biological aunt) I was always reassured of my prettiness and how I would grow up to be the most beautiful girl in the world.

When I went to live with my mom a couple years later, I didn't hear that I was pretty or gorgeous as much as

I did when I lived with my mama, but I knew I was pretty without hearing it. There is this one picture that I have that made me start to question my beauty. I used to have a Pitbull dog name Max-A-Million, he was jet black and so beautiful. I have a photo of me and Max standing in the backyard, it was at night, so it was dark outside. In the picture all you really see is the pink roller in my hair, my blue and white striped shirt and our teeth. When I first saw the picture as a child it made me laugh because Max and I was so dark you didn't even see us. I later found this same picture to bring tears to my eyes for the same reason it made me laugh.

At the age of 8 years old, my mom and I moved to a predominately Caucasian neighborhood, we lived in a complex building of about twenty or so buildings. The schools in this neighborhood had school bus service that stopped at every building to take us to and from school every day. It wasn't until I had to ride this bus, that I would question my beauty. Growing up the "dark skin girl" was so heartbreaking... I can remember being the only dark-skinned black girl in my class. Being teased for being black and dark. Then to add icing on the cake, not only was I dark skinned but I also had buck teeth. Could it have been any worse? I doubt it...

I can remember being teased and taunted daily, about the way I looked. I was dark, very skinny, flat as a board as they would say. I had buck teeth; I sucked my thumb from the age of 6 years old until I was 18. I thought that I had been born sucking my thumb but it wasn't until adulthood that I found out that I was actually 6 years old when I started to suck my thumb to cope with trauma. My hair was often *"nappy looking"*; my mother would press it on a Sunday and comb it, if I got it wet during the week, I would have to wait until it was hair day again to get it *"fixed"*.

From the age of 8 years old to the age of maybe 12 or 13 years old, I was talked about, teased taunted and bullied. At first it was the Caucasian kids that would tease, taunt, bully, and even beat me up. Yes, every Friday, like clockwork I would get off the school bus at my building, and the hitting, spitting, kicking, and very hurtful words would begin, until either they got tired or almost caught by an adult. Those Friday beatings didn't end until I stood up for myself by carrying a knife back and forth to school, (also got my mom and I evicted from the apartment as well).

After that, my mom and I moved to a neighborhood were all the kids looked like me, however, now I am the *"skinny ugly burnt kid"* that nobody wanted on their team in gym class. I teased yet again, teased, taunted and hated even by my own kind… How? Why? What made me so different from everyone else? I just couldn't understand it.

I remember the day I met my biological father, my brother walked me to his apartment (yeah, you need to go back to the first book, *"The Letter, From the Invisible Daughter"* if you are unsure of how I met my dad), my father opened the door and said *"hey, black gal"*, I literally almost died standing at that door. I just remember thinking "how could you call me that, how could you too tease me about my skin color? Aren't I the same color as you are?" I felt so crushed to be the black gal. It wasn't until my adult years my father told me how it was never his intention to hurt my feelings, to him the term black gal was a term of endearment. To him it was the same as saying hey pretty girl. Because my dad is from the South, I definitely can see this being very true for him.

I truly believe, that being called ugly, being called black girl, being called monkey, gorilla, and all the horrible derogatory hateful names growing up caused me to not believe in ME. Subconsciously, I never really put the root cause of my insecurities and being teased together. As a teenager I found myself wanting to just be loved, I didn't care if I was actually liked or not. If that makes any sense at all. By suppressing these feeling about myself and my image, it molded the way that I allowed myself and others to treat me. Because I felt as if I was the ugly duckling, I never truly felt good enough, never cute enough... that's a horrible feeling to have at a very young age. At age 9, a girl is supposed to feel like a princess, she should feel as if the world is rooting for her; yet I felt the complete opposite. This feeling followed me well into my late adulthood.

The day I decided that I was tired of being sad, tired of being the "ugly duckling", tired of feeling unlovable, I made the decision to look at myself in the mirror. I took the time to look at ME, the naked me... The me with no makeup, no "*mask*", just me... all me! I had to teach myself how to love me. I had to date myself, take care of myself. I truly had to do the work to heal myself from myself first. I started therapy sessions to talk about my traumas as well as talking about my own thoughts of me and how they were just as detrimental as what others said and thought about me.

For me doing the work to heal is what made my relationship with God even stronger. Reading his word, the one thing (there were several but for the sake of this chapter, we will talk about the scriptures above) that stuck with me is, I am made in HIS image so how can I be ugly, my Father is not ugly, He is perfectly made, therefore so am I. I live my life today on top of the world. Knowing that I am beautiful in my skin. Nope I may not be everyone's "cup of tea" however, I am my own cup of tea and sometimes coffee. I love me from the top of my head to the soles of my feet.

I now teach my daughters how to love themselves no matter what. My youngest daughter in 9 years old now and she is er happiest when she has her hair in its most natural state in a ponytail with the biggest "nappiest" puff spilling out of the top. I teach her that she doesn't have "nappy" hair, she has beautiful coils that are sometimes just a little kinky. I teach her to smile bright and know that her smile brightens even the darkest of rooms. I teach her that her body is a temple and should be honored daily, with beautiful affirmations. I make sure that no matter how the outside world treats her she must treat herself better. So, at 9 years old, she knows she wears an invisible crown, the moment she walks sad, or holds her head down in self-image shame the crown can fall off. She says to me all the time, "oh no Mommy, I can't walk with my head down, my crown cost too much to hit the ground". To many that may not seem like much, but for me, that statement says much more than "*money*". That statement, says to me, that she knows that there is a "cost" associated with loosing yourself because of someone else's thoughts of you.

To you... the person that may read this, I want you to know that no matter what happens, no matter what "they" may say... Keep your head high, you never want your crown to fall off and hit the ground.... The cost is way to great!!! Know that you are more than JUST your skin!

Because I Am More Than JUST My Skin

Chapter Two

Created A

Masterpiece

Nina Motivates

Nina Monique Thomas, was born the 9th child to the blended family of Audrey and Freeman Pendleton. Nina was born and raised in Chicago. Nina was born unique to her family, being the only known immediate family member to be born with a physical difference. Nina was born with a condition called "club hands". Meaning, her thumbs were removed due to lack of bones, and her arms did not properly develop. This has not stopped her from accomplishing greatness!

Nina received her Bachelors of Science in Human Development and Family Studies at the University of Illinois at Urbana-Champaign, and studied Social Work at Loyola University in Chicago.

Nina has a passion for youth and young adults. Because of her great love for youth and desire to help build them, Nina continue to develop programs specifically for youth to build youth of today.

In 2012 Nina became a certified Christian Life Breakthrough Coach through the Life Breakthrough Academy. In February 2013 Nina released her first of many paperback books titled "Because I Love Me." Nina served as the Chicago South SPAA (Speakers, Publishers & Authors Association) President for 2013. She won the speaker of the year for SPAA in 2013. Nina took 2014 by storm by becoming the co-host of "Own My Own" talk radio show, co-host of Motivating the Motivators weekly empowerment call, wrote on "Mental Stability" for Speak It News Online Magazine, and was the host of the Gospel Gossip Entertainment Television show! Nina was also ordained as an Evangelist in September of 2014.

June 2015, Nina combined her skills as a motivator with her gift to make people laugh and became a comedic motivator. She began performing and traveling not only motivating, but bringing laughter into the lives of many!

In the late summer of 2016 Nina launched Anointed Hands Publishing Company. One of the ways Nina use her coaching certification is by coaching bloggers and authors to take their writing ideas off their minds and onto the web and into books!

In December of 2017, Nina took her passion of baking and created Nina Boo Sweets. Nina Boo Sweets is your ticket to butter cookie heaven. December 2018 Nina expanded Nina Boo Sweets and added organic healthy teas and organic coffee. Nina was ordained a Pastor of Youth at Be Whole Christian Center in March of 2018.

With several businesses and services, Nina was then branded as the Xtreme Entrepreneur. Nina has traveled to several states speaking life, sent cookies and teas all over, and plan to continue traveling and expanding her gifts.

By January 2020, Nina had published ten of her own books and several client books. Nina launched Book Writing 101, teaching others how to write and publish books. By March 2020 Nina began working on her first book collaboration "You Can: 33 Stories to Uplift & Inspire Everyday

People." The book launched August 1st 2020 and sold over 500 books in the first month. Nina is continuing to put together book collaborations and workshops to help more people, youth and adults, become published authors.

Although Nina first passion is inspiring and coaching youth, she uses all her gifts daily. "I will leave this world empty of all the gifts within me!"

To connect with Nina, please visit www.ninamotivates.info or email coachninmotivates@gmail.com

Created A Masterpiece

India Arie said it best in her hit song "I am Not my hair," when she said " I am not my skin, I and not your expectations no.... I am the soul that lives within." Whew, how true are those words to me? Very true! From a young child I had to take this stance. I could not be my skin, hair, shape etc. I am a black disabled female. The odds were instantly stacked against me from birth.

I was born different. I was born with "club hands." This means I was born without bones in my thumbs, arms are short, curvy and I had to have a total of 6 surgeries. I have Full movement in my right hand, limited movement in my left hand. At the age of 39, I still have scars from my surgery that will never go away. Having this "*difference*" brought on so many obstacles. The journey of being "*different*" started as a little girl.

It wasn't until I went to public school for the first time that I noticed people looked at me different. I had to be around 5 or 6 years old at the time. I came from a huge family, and everyone treated me normal, so I was okay with being "normal." However, out in the world, people would stare at me. They would run from me. Some even made weird noises as if they were afraid of me. They told me they were sorry for my "difference." People would come up with mean names like four finger Nina, smurf, and alien. People were so mean. Not just children my age, but adults would be mean also. I remember an instance where I was on the CTA (Chicago Transit Authority) and the bus driver would not open the door to the bus because he wanted me to tell him what happened to my hands. You wouldn't believe the issues I faced just by looking different. Matter of a fact, just by having a small physical difference.

Even the Chicago Public School system thought that my hands looking different meant I needed special help in school. My parents had to fight for me to attend public school. I remember going to all these appointments, not knowing what they were at the time. Now I know, I was being tested to see if I had a learning disability. I passed all their test with flying colors and was able to attend public school with no special accommodations.

There was a season in my life where I only wore long sleeve shirts so that I was not starred at or bullied. I wanted a break. I got tired of people looking at me as if I was not human. I just had something more visibly different than most people. It wasn't until my sister proved to me that everyone was different, that I became more comfortable being me and loving the skin I was in. She told me to go look at my bullies and I would see a difference with them too. I sure did. One boy was what we called crossed eyed. One girl was being bullied so she became the bully. Sometimes people are cruel because they do not know how to channel their pain in a proper way. I dealt with this often.

I had to go through a total mind and heart makeover in order to love the skin that I am in. Once I did that, I was able to live comfortable just the way I am. It was not easy. My foundation in loving me was first, growing in God.

This had to start as a child. I started going to church at the age of 8 years old; I began to love God and the good things His word said about me. When I began to read things in the Holy Bible that said I was the apple of God's eye, fearfully and wonderfully made and that He knew me before I was formed in my mother's womb, I begin to love me more. If I am to believe God, I must believe what He says about me. I must know that He had a purpose for making me the way He made me! This made me a determined person. I began to allow the things people said I could not do, push me to doing them.

When I got to high school, I decided I would not let my difference stop me from doing anything I desired to do. I joined the cheerleading team, JROTC (Jr Reserve Officer Training Corp), and so many other things. I refused to allow my skin/difference to hinder me. Many times, people thought I was crazy for trying new things. Then, when they would see that I not only tried things, but conquered them, they began to believe in themselves even more. What was supposed to be a situation to break me down, I allowed it to build me up. My skin/difference became my greatest characteristic.

God has made us all different. No two people are the same. We are all different. We are different colors, shapes, sizes etc. We cannot compare ourselves to others. In this book we are talking about skin, but people often struggle with many other things. When I was not comfortable in my skin, it brought on insecurities. Insecurities bring on bad decisions. Even as an adult I had a time where I struggled. Struggling loving my skin, my hands, got me into trouble when dating. Honestly, it took time for me to even realize that my own insecurities were the problem.

This showed up in dating situations. I would be with a guy I know I should have not been with but would stay with him. I would come up with so many reasons why I should stay, even when it made no sense. I remember a man told me his wife asked him if he thought I would ever get married. He said he told her, well someone married you didn't they. That was so funny to me. Fact is, she thought no one would marry me because of my hands. Quickly fast forward to where my life is now, I will be married in about 45 days. Now back to the past....

Once I started dating, I got comfortable with a guy and his family and I did not want to start over. This caused me to stay in relationships that I should not have been in. How did this relate to the skin I was in? Well, if I was comfortable with my hands, I would not have been worried about being accepted. I did not want to have to explain to another family what happened to my hands, so I would settle. This caused me a lot of unnecessary pain. I dealt with domestic violence due to this mindset. Many people often think domestic violence is only physical abuse. No! Domestic violence also includes mental and financial abuse. I was more so mentally abused. I was called names, cheated on, had mind tricks played on me, just to name a few. I was financially abused as well. This abuse made me depressed. Sometimes you can have the desire to just be loved, not realizing you must first start to love yourself just the way you are. I had to go back to the mentality that I had growing up. My hands are unique and I do not have to settle. I had to make that stand in all areas. Once I did that, I stop accepting less than I deserved, even in relationships.

I had to grab the mindset that my skin or shall I say my physical difference did not make me. I made me. Yes, I was and will always be different. That is okay. There are times I had to remind myself that my uniqueness is needed in the world. I still have to remind myself of this. Am I accepted everywhere I go? No! Do people still stare? Yes! This is something I may deal with for the rest of my life. I, however, must stay comfortable with me. I must love me. I must value my skin. When you value and love you just the way you are, others begin to do so too.

I learned to be consistent with self-love. It could not be a seasonal thing. It had to be overall. Maintaining my joy with self takes daily work. Whenever insecurities try to creep up, I have to remind myself who I am in God. I remind myself that He created me for and with purpose just the way I am. He did not create me for me not to love me. My difference is meant to make a difference. I am meant to stand out. Yes, this black disabled female is meant to leave a stamp in the world. That is why I have decided to strive daily to love the skin I am in and live in purpose on purpose! Again, as India Arie says, I am not my skin, I am the soul that lives within. I encourage you, the reader, to remind yourself just how special you are daily. You are fearfully and wonderfully made. Love the skin you are in!

Because I Am More Than JUST My Skin

Chapter Three

Black and Beautiful

KeiSha Osgood

Ms. KeiSha E. Osgood is a native of Savannah, Georgia who grew up in a 'Blended and Extended Family,' along with her brother William. Their mother, Stacy, is a Retired Naval Officer, which afforded them an opportunity to live and travel abroad, as well as in various regions in the United States. KeiSha has a Degree and Credentials in Early Childhood Education. She is dedicated to educating young children and motivating them to expand their horizons through the fundamentals of Mathematics, Reading, Science and other areas of Academia. In addition, she hopes to someday own and operate an Inspirational Cafe' where patrons can enjoy live music, poetry and inspirational readings in a relaxing atmosphere.

KeiSha is a Commercial and Runway Model, as well as a Fashion Stylist. Musically gifted and talented, she plays the Violin, Cello and Flute. She enjoys listening to all genres of music, dancing, singing, reading and creative writing. She is an International Best-Selling Author who enjoys writing Poetry and short stories for children. She is a Black Belt in Tae Kwon Do and from Middle School through College, she competed in the 200-meter and 400-meter Relay Races on the Track and Field Team. Today, she continues to compete in charity events. She has received numerous Academic and Athletic Accolades and a Guinness World Record - as one of 5,003 participants in the PodFest Global Summit, the world's largest attendance for a one-week Virtual Conference in August 2020.

KeiSha is most thankful for her 'Blended and Extended Family' and honors the 'Village' that helped inspire her to be the woman she is today. Her professional affiliations include: Girls Scouts of America; Boys and Girls Clubs of America; Athletes Against Drugs (AAD); 'Toots for Books' Literacy Foundation; Professional Woman Network and National Association for the Education of Young Children (NAEYC). She is active in her Church and in her community. To God Be the Glory!

Black and Beautiful

Sitting on the loveseat in my living room listening to music and looking through the pages of the family photo albums, I was reminded of how in most of the pictures...I am darker than everyone else. Even my childhood pictures show that I have a dark complexion. As I turned the pages, reflecting over snapshots of my life, a lot of painful memories from my past rose to the surface...

I remember as a little girl, going to Surfside Elementary School in Chula Vista, California; a very beautiful city outside of San Diego. I lived there with my mother, Stacy, who was in the Navy and stationed there at the time, my 'Bonus Dad', Willie, and my baby brother, William. The Elementary School that I attended was predominantly Caucasian and Hispanic students, probably due to the location. Sure, there were several different ethnicities there but when it came to African-Americans...I was often 'the only one.' I remember one particular day, a girl named Susie walked up to me in class and said, "Why are you so black?" I was caught-off guard by her question because I always knew I was black BUT I did not pay much attention to the fact that I was *SO* black, as she had pointed out. From that day forward, I struggled with self-image and self-esteem issues.

My mother and I had conversations about my looks and how others teased me. I told her that I did not like my looks because I was not able to make or keep friends because of them. She reassured me of my beauty and talked to me about our African Ancestry, as well as the history of my father's (Keith) family. I was young and did not understand everything that she explained to me but she made me feel special. She made me feel very pretty.

By the time I was in Middle School, my mother was stationed in Bethesda, Maryland and we lived in the city of Landover. When I was a Junior High Student at Parkland Middle School, I was not picked on as much by my Caucasian schoolmates. By then, the teasing by them was almost non-existent and I was feeling better about myself. I was blossoming into a beautiful young lady and I was frequently getting compliments about my looks. Ironically, it was now my African-American school mates that were rejecting me because of my dark skin. Many of them would look at me and frown. Some would whisper amongst themselves, while looking at me and pointing. Others would tease me and call me names like 'Blackie' and 'Midnight.' A few went so far as to call me a 'Tranny' making reference to me having possibly been a boy who was becoming or pretending to be a girl instead.

One day, I was on my way to a class and stopped at a water fountain for a drink. The hallway was crowded with students rushing back and forth. Another student, an African-American boy, was walking by and pushed my head down into the fountain. He pushed my head so hard that my mouth hit the fountain's spout and my top lip was cut. I stood there embarrassed as others watched and laughed. No one came to my rescue. I stood there bleeding and no one bothered to ask if I was okay. I covered my mouth and rushed to the nearest Girls' restroom to clean my mouth and make sure none of my teeth were broken. There was a lot of blood and I was in a lot of pain. After washing my mouth out, and washing away the tears from my face, I caught a glimpse of myself in the mirror. I wanted to turn away but instead, I stood there, staring at my reflection. I saw what others saw: dark skin, high cheekbones, pearly white teeth and deep-set eyes. For the very first time, I noticed that my skin had no blemishes. In fact, it was flawless. And, my teeth were set perfectly. I liked what I saw and I decided, right then and there, to accept me as I was - even if no one else did. And, I was determined to love me - even if no one else did.

From that day forward, the African-American students seemed to avoid me even more. They did not talk to me. They did not invite me to sit with them in the school cafeteria during lunch or to socialize with them. Nor, did they invite me to parties, gatherings or other fun activities. I was isolated and I felt alone. I thought to myself... *"Wow... Even my own people do not accept me."* Every now and then, one or more of them would yell out to me saying, *"Light skin is the right skin."* I mean...really? Who makes that determination? Well...I supposed they did. But it did not matter to me. Despite the teasing, bullying and rejection, I had the best kind of love that exists: self-love!

By the time I entered High School, the color lines began to blur. By then, my mother was stationed in Norfolk, Virginia and we lived about thirty minutes away in the city of Chesapeake. I was in a school with a more diverse student population and more of my schoolmates were African-American. I got along with them, for the most part, but it was a struggle. I remembered the hurtful things that some of my schoolmates said to me in Middle School. I saw quite a few familiar faces because some of my schoolmates were also 'Military Brats' (a term of endearment for children in Military Families). So, some of them ended up at Deer Creek High School, along with me. And, when they invited me to join them for social gatherings, I was not sure if they were being sincere. Sure, they were friendly enough but I did not forget how cruel they were to me in previous years. Yes, we were older now but their words still affected me. In the back of my mind, I often heard the following words echo... *"Sticks and stones may break my bones but words will never hurt me."* Whoever came up with *that* saying apparently had no idea the deep, emotional wounds that words *can* inflict on others.

One Saturday morning, my mother and I were enjoying one of our favorite pastimes: strolling through the Green Gate Mall in Chesapeake. A woman approached me and asked, *"What Modeling Agency represents you?"* I looked at her and replied, *"None. Right now I am a Senior in High School and I plan to go to college to study Early Childhood Education. I love children and I help my parents with my brother. I am not a Model but I love clothes and I hope to be a Fashion Stylist someday."* Then I thought to myself, *"Is she serious?"* She gave me her card and invited me to a Model Casting Call for an upcoming Runway Show. Ms. Tia Wilkes was her name. She complimented me on my *'Strikingly Unique'* features, as she called them. She continued speaking but I was stunned at her interest in me as I stood there listening to her speak. And although I was surprised at how free flowing her compliments were, her words were like music to my ears. After about twenty minutes of getting acquainted, Ms. Tia Wilkes, my mother and I exchanged a few choruses of,

"See you soon." "Until we meet again." and *"It was a pleasure meeting you."* - we all went on about our day. As my mom and I continued walking through the Mall, I thought to myself, *"Is she serious?"* I smiled inside as we stopped at Forever 21, one of my favorite stores.

A few months later, I was backstage at the Rimaldi Fashion House for my big debut at New York Fashion Week. Several other Models and I were preparing for the largest, international fashion event of the year. A-List Celebrities and the 'Who's Who' of the fashion world were seated front and center. And, soon, I would be strutting down the catwalk for all the world to see. I was making my Runway debut in a stunning Afrocentric Ensemble designed by Ms. Niko, an amazing Fashion Designer.

As I stood at the end of the catwalk waiting for my music to play, I inhaled deeply, closed my eyes and prayed silently. Then, I heard the voice of the Nigerian Singer, Chinedu Okoli, who goes by the stage name of Flavour N'abania or simply Flavour. He is also a songwriter and multi-instrumentalist who began his musical career as a drummer for a local church. His sultry voice started booming through the loudspeaker, filling the room with a powerful Afro-rhythm, and the words of his empowerment anthem *"Black Is Beautiful!"* With a wide, bright smile, I took to the runway with my head held high as the crowd cheered me on. I felt proud and happy to be ME! Flavour's words inspired me...

"I can see her from afar. She just shines like a morning light.

I can see very clearly. She just shines in a broad daylight.

And she was walking. And I was watching every step and the moves she was making.

She is adoring. I am admiring her hips. Her beauty is a natural thing,

An original thing and a mysterious thing... I raise up my voice and sing.

I thank the Lord for a beauty Queen. 'Cause your black is beautiful.

Beauty from my own. Baby, your black is beautiful.

You are a beauty in disguise. And your black is beautiful.

Black is beautiful. And your black is natural. Black is original.

She is black, she is proud and she knows it. She is cool and everybody likes it.

She is bold and she is very, very humble. She is strong and can never, never fumble.

She is courageous. Her smile's contagious. She's the kind of woman I can take for serious.

Beauty is a natural thing, an original thing and a mysterious thing.

I raise up my voice and sing. I thank the Lord for a beauty Queen.

'Cause your black is beautiful. Baby, your black is beautiful. Beauty in disguise.

Your black is Africa. Your black is Jamaica.

Because I Am More Than JUST My Skin

Your black is Arabia. Your black is Jamaica.

And your black is Nigeria.....Your black is beautiful.

Your black is beautiful."

Today, I am working as a Licensed and Credentialed Early Childhood Educator. Of course, since I grew up in a Military Family, it should come as no surprise that I work at the Childcare Development Center (CDC) on a Navy Base. My love for children inspired my career choice. I thank my brother, William, for that. Being his 'Big Sister' and helping my parents look after him when he was young was such a joy.

As for my Modeling career, I get opportunities to showcase my fashion skills quite frequently. My photographs can be found in several magazines and editorial print media all around the world. My Personal Photographer, Katoria, looks through the lens of her camera and inspires me to empower others to accept themselves for who they are. And, every now and then, you may even see me strutting down a catwalk in New York City; Miami, Florida; Los Angeles, California; Chicago, Illinois; Atlanta, Georgia or in some exotic locations overseas. No matter where you see me, I am easy to recognize. I am tall and slender - with a stride like a gazelle. My head is held high - as I look toward the heavens. My naturally dark melanin is kissed by the sun. My smile reflects the beauty of my Ancestors. I am KeiSha. And, I proudly represent Mother Africa in all of her splendor. Yes, I am Black and Beautiful, inside and out. I Am More Than *JUST* My Skin!

Chapter Four

From Self-Consciousness to Self ... Enlightenment to Self-Love

Alicia Hall

Alicia Hall…. My primary goal in counseling is to help others regain hope for a future filled with a sense of identity, spirituality, morality, self-acceptance, self-worth and overall happiness. That is my divine purpose and I strive daily towards those efforts. While walking my purpose, I attained formal education from University Of Missouri St. Louis where I gained my BA in Psychology, M.Ed. In Clinical Mental Health Counseling w emphasis in Integrative treatment from CACREP Accredited program. I also attained Degree in Non-Profit Management and Leadership (NPML) in Public Policy & Management. I am a Nationally Certified Counselor (NCC) and Licensed Professional Counselor (LPC). Currently I'm the owner and lead clinician at SkiWise Behavioral Health & Wellness Services with the goal of proving training and culturally intelligence to up and coming clinical professionals. But above all, I am a child of God & Sapphire's Grandbaby.

Moto:

Hymn: 'If I can help somebody, then my living shall not be in vein'. Mahalia Jackson

From Self-Consciousness to Self ... Enlightenment to Self-Love

I didn't like the name, buckwheat or black beauty!

Growing up as a child, people didn't realize how fragile the young mind was and in the 70's it definitely wasn't understood. For me, as a child at the time, I held my elders in high regard. I never realized how their words would have such an impact on my development and self-esteem.

Buckwheat was my nickname given to me by my grandfather. The 'Buckwheat' I knew was a lil kid, who was bright eyed, with nappy unkept pick-tails. He wore raggedy tattered clothes, who seemed to be mentally delayed, that had the skin color of black tar. That was me.... that's what he saw when he looked at me... Buckwheat. He wasn't a malicious, nor a mean man, he was just my grandpa who nicknamed all the kids, and I was called Buckwheat.

Around the age five, while watching The Lil Rascals tv show, I was brought face to face with my namesake. I saw who I was named in the likeness of and it was at that time I began to realize the differences in me. I was different cause I was a black tar baby, whom was to be deemed a bafoon, for people to ridicule based on the darker shade of my skin and nappy hair. It was then I began to see my difference from my family and what they thought of me, *not to mention how they treated other light skinned grandchildren born in the family.*

As I approached my teen years, the nickname changed from Buckwheat to... Black Beauty. Well guess what? Black beauty was.... a black horse that nobody liked, made fun of, and looked at with disdain. A black unwanted horse. That wasn't better. This became a self-fulfilling prophecy.

Beauty... it's all a matter of perspective. What one sees... You may not feel... and what you feel... others definitely can't see.

My Family Makeup

I began to believe that the darker a person was, the more hardship one experienced from their own kind. Light skin was better than being dark skinned. And dark to black skin was seen as bad, ugly, or undesirable.

I began to ask my mom, "how was it that I was the only dark-skinned person in our family?" My mama side of the family, is light skinned because, my grandmother was Native American with associated features. A very demure and beautiful woman with a flawless light-colored skin complexion, and shiny, wavy, luxurious, long hair. And my maternal grandfather was a biracial man, with a light skinned mother and a white father, which allowed him the privilege of passing for white in many social circles.

I mention this to show how all their children, including my mother, were born light, bright with good hair, and trademark of a green booty birthmark.

She developed a liking to finding a dark-skinned black man, to be able to have a dark skinned, chocolate baby, and she did. My father is a tall, slim, handsome black man, with strong textured hair worn in a tall Afro.

Enters the... Black Frog w White Eyes!

So, I was born according to my mother's desire to have a dark-skinned baby. I was the first Grandbaby born into this light bright family... a dark-skinned child. I was told endearingly, that I was a cute black frog with white, bright eyes!!!! Cute... but different cause I was dark.

Oh my, they loved on me like a chocolate drop. I was dressed up, paraded around, cuddled and really embraced as the lil black cutie that I was. Always referred to, by my bright eyes and dark skinned. I was the only chocolate baby amongst all the lighter skinned grandchildren for years. So, when they called for Buckwheat... everyone knew who they were talking about... Me.

I had become self-conscious. I began to get quiet and hide within as if my blackness would help me to fade out. I hated being called buckwheat! I hated what it stood for; it was the self-defining name given to me. My cousins also had nicknames, but I felt I had the most horrible name of them all. And it hurt. Not to mention, other family members thought the name was funny, however, I lacked the humor of it.

I was feeling like a black frog, with bright eyes, who looked like buckwheat yet was treated like black beauty. I was feeling undesirable and ugly; how I felt about it, started to show in my behavior. I began to act angry, withdrawn, with bad attitude that showed all in my face and demeanor. I had such low self-esteem. I became obsessed with being different all because I hated my dark-skinned complexion.

As if things couldn't get worse, then came the pimples and spots on my skin. As I moved through childhood with these poor self-perceptions, I worried about it so much so that I was thrown into early teenage puberty with severe acne, all over my face and body. The pimples were puss filled, skin was inflamed and it left scars. Then on top of that, I got chicken pops in high school which left me polka dotted.

This caused public ridicule, taunting and bullying from my peers in school. The girls talked about me so bad that I found myself fighting or skipping school to avert from problems. I started to not go outside and play with friends even though they would come get me. My family would comment on the severity of my skin inflammation. I went to several Dr. to treat skin dysfunction only to get sicker from the medication they would prescribe. And yet nothing helped.

As a result, along with other childhood traumatic experiences, I began to act out. I didn't see or feel any self-value or self-worth. I hated it and I hated myself. When I looked in the mirror, I saw... a black monster.

I began to obsess about my appearance. I was constantly attempting to "cover-up" the affected area with globs of chemicals and makeup. I avoided social situations due to perceived defects. I began a toxic habit of comparing myself to others, being envious and jealous. I spent significant amounts of time fixating on perceived flaws. I began to become an introvert. I became super quiet and stand-offish, trying to fade into being invisible to others. I lost my voice, my confidence, in fear of my flaws being seen.

I didn't like attention, in any form, for fear of being noticed for my abnormalities. I isolated from others and spent hours alone, locked in the bathroom, working on the removal of pimples, skin scrubbing and applying various products promising skin clearing and lightening. There were recurring appointments with professionals on how to "fix" perceived flaw. On into adulthood, I began the journey into repeated cosmetic and/or plastic surgeries, regardless of risk or expense. I didn't care. I wanted to look beautiful... to me and to others.

Sapphire's Baby (Journey to Self-Discovery)

My grandmother, who was called Sapphire, picked up on my sadness and internal turmoil. She began to talk to me. She would always check in with how I was feeling. She let me know she could SEE how I was feeling by my low demeanor. I shared with her vaguely how I felt *"different"*. One day she said something so profound...

"it's hard to love a child that hates themselves". That shocked me that she could see the self-hatred on the outside of me. She went further to say, "Sapphire don't have any ugly babies!" My grandma, taught me that 'beauty is what you feel about yourself, not about what other people think of you or what you see in the mirror. Learning to love yourself will be the hardest thing that you ever do. But when you do fall in love with self it will be the most amazing feeling ever, for which your overall beauty will emanate from within.'

At that point I begin to learn about my hang ups and misperceptions. I was always smart and loved to research things I didn't understand. So, I delve into learning about me. I began to try to understand why I had such a level of hatred for my darker colored skin complexion.

I suffered from Body Dysmorphic Disorder (BDD). This is a sickness where I became obsessed with defects in my appearance which in turn made me suffer from childhood depression leading to adulthood obsessive disorder. Having BDD negatively affected my relationships and interactions.

I would be worrying that I was "a freak" and / or "unlovable." I knew my family loved me very much, but I was terrified of other people's perception of me. With this came being bullied, sexual abuse, and other life situations that changed my perspective of myself, my world, and my place in it, all of which are symptoms of trauma. This caused paranoia and obsession which too was a sickness, leading to constant thoughts of self-hatred and suicidal thinking. Body dysmorphia caused me to have severe emotional distress, triggering my anxiety, low self-esteem, depression, and more.

It has taken a lot for me to even take pictures... let alone post pictures of myself... because I was thinking that people could see my soul... and of what I knew about my soul... it was not pretty. I remember my cousin asking me why I hated taking pictures? I told her, when I see myself in pictures... I see a monster. She thought that was so awkward and we never mentioned it again.

Meaning Making of Beauty!

So now that I had a better understanding of my circumstances, I continued to reflect on my grandmother's words regarding self-love. What in fact, if anything, did I love about myself?

I was super smart, a straight 'A' student, who was in Probe and Honors classes through school years. I could play the piano and read sheet music so well! I was responsible and a great caretaker. I was a kind and good person. I was a great helper and loved working with kids. I was a great swimmer and very adventurous. I could skate my buns off... I mean with the best of them. I loved my family and was always there for them when needed and/or wanted. I was a great mother, stepmom and caregiver to my little cousins. I was a good person. I *AM* a good person. I was beautiful... on the inside, regardless of what I looked like on the outside.

What I had to learn to do was SMILE. I remember an instance where I was on the school bus, trying really hard not to be seen, this girl told a joke and I laughed out loud. She stopped in the middle of everything and said, "you have a beautiful smile!" I was floored. I looked at her with much confusion. I went home and looked in the mirror for hours... looking at my smile. She was right. I had a contagious smile with super white teeth. Even to this day people will comment on my smile and I have to pause to tell myself... *"yes, you do have a beautiful smile"*.

In my journey from *"Buckwheat to Black Beauty"*, I learned that:

Buckwheat was one of the most beloved characters in the history of the Our Gang and Little Rascals films. He rose from obscurity to become an American icon. Producer Hal Roach, Sr. picked three-year-old "Buckwheat" from hundreds of children and raised him on a pedestal before an adoring public. For a decade, Buckwheat was the most prominent Black American in motion pictures. Buckwheat achieved a lasting legacy with many enjoying the timeless tale of a baby superstar.

Black Beauty story describes both the cruelty and kindness that an ebony-colored horse experiences through his lifetime. Black Beauty illustrates the importance of kindness and civility even during hardships, ridicule and judgement. Black Beauty, as his name suggests, was prized for his size and strength. Though still beautiful, Black Beauty encounters several situations that tested his values and perceptions while at the same time built his character, courage and dedication far beyond vanity. This resulted in

Black Beauty being the most honored example of humility and beauty.

As I continue on this journey of self-discovery, I did, as Sapphire stated, I begin to fall in Love with myself. My beautiful dark skin, every pimple and polka dot that comes and goes, my nappy hair (even though I prefer weave), my body (even though I still struggle with my perceptions of it), my style and finesse. But what I truly love about the skin I'm in is that, I'm a great person, I live to enhance the lives of others and that brings me purpose and internal joy. My living is not in vein or vanity, it is in my ability to help others along their journey of self-discovery and hopefully... self-acceptance and love.

Now... at the age of 49... I'm coming to terms with a lot of things. And one of those major things is... I am beautiful! Both inside and out! No longer second guessing myself or placing value in others opinions of me. No longer allowing myself to be hostage or victim of circumstances. Planning my steps, walking my path... and further staying in my lane while being aware of dead ends. I want happiness, joy and self-love for everyone I encounter... it's my life's work! But more importantly... I want it and I am embracing it for myself. With that, please know... I am loving the skin that I am in!!!

Because I Am More Than JUST My Skin

Chapter Five

Keys, Crown, Melanated Skin & Glory

Q.R. Williams-Oakes

Q.R. Williams-Oakes Co-author, Q.R. Williams-Oakes truly has a passion for written word and anything that carries an exuberant level of positivity. In 2019, she solidified being the owner of Epiphany Expression LLC; a business that assists with creative writing and notary services. She is currently the Senior Administrative Assistant for a health plan management company. She is certified as a Community Health Worker and Mental Health First Aid Advocate. She recently obtained certification in Restorative Justice 101. Q.R. is a constant supporter of social services. She is also the co-author of the books, 'After We Parted: Rebuilding Our Lives After Divorce' and 'It's a Matron of Honor: Journey to Womanhood'.

"There is only one you; Might as well get comfortable representing that one unique vessel. Manning your ship is important because it house everything that you are and will ever become. There will also be moments when you have to mend it."

Q.R. desires for you to be self-aware, accountable and proud of your very being.

"May your corium carry a glow and your heart be filled with unspeakable joy."

Epiphany Expression LLC
epiphanyexpression@gmail.com

Keys, Crown, Melanated Skin & Glory

What is your anthem? It's your personal theme song or soundtrack to your life. Let it play! When you are getting dressed or stepping out of the house, a song about how you feel may come to mind. If you are obsessed with music like I am, you have a song for every feeling and every moment. 'Living My Life like it's Golden' by Jill Scott or 'Walking' by Mary Mary; along with a few other songs fit so well. Those songs reflect my vibe and just puts a smile on my face. When you are feeling fabulous, dressed to the nine or not even dressed at all; I hope you have your head held high with confidence and strength, like you are a foxy lady strutting with power in a scene from a 70's blaxploitation flick. So often we create the soundtrack of our lives. What songs will echo through? Far as my awkward yet beautiful sway; If I had to press play on my life's boom box (with what I call the Bobby 'Blue' Bland Speakers); I am sure 'The Makings of You' by Curtis Mayfield and 'Adore' by Prince would be blaring out, following me in surround sound. If you haven't selected a song by now, choose one and listen to it for just a moment.

Abba created you to be different. You were created using a unique mold. Why would you ever try to forcefully fit or insert yourself in a place that doesn't hug your curves or reflect your silhouette? Our differences are the things that house our purpose, gifts and everything we were meant to receive or give. We have the keys to unlock and access so much. We have the keys to change our own narrative and the way we view ourselves.

Images... What do you see? Visually this is your own personal concept of "you". It is a picture you have painted; it is your truth. It should highlight your statuesque beauty. Some of what you feel about yourself is partially due to others' perception of you or the words they've spoken. How do you develop an image of self that refrain from outside influences that diminish the core you? Getting to a place of having a transparent image of self is critical. What would you say about you? As I look back over how I view myself, as far as an outward appearance; there are definite moment's that orchestrated or defined what I saw on the outer layer of my temple. I am a vessel that carry this shell and the representation of it is important. What image do I want to project when I come into view for others to see?

The vision of self is created early on. I know that from my experiences and looking in the eyes of our youth. As they say, "out of the mouth of babes". My niece, Antania loves taking pictures. One day, we were taking a picture together using my cell phone, she asked with excitement, "Can I see it?" She immediately proclaimed, "I'm cute!" Those have been words of affirmation for me ever since; in the exact way that she said it with so much happiness and reassurance. It's okay to allow a lens to focus on your beauty, capturing the reflections of you within that moment.

I reflect to a time when I was around my niece's age; daddy telling mama, "Don't put that "conkalina" (perm) in that girl's hair." He wanted me to embrace my natural beauty. A woman's [in this case, girl's] crown is her glory, right? No, I didn't have naturally tamable curls as he did. Always looking at him as having good hair. I grew older to embrace and love my coils. Black hair *is* good hair; no matter the texture or the length. Mama was just saving me from ridicule because fros and kinks just weren't something that was seen often in the early 90's. I am so glad we as a people are getting back to the place of embracing everything the exude being black; melanated and all, we literally carry the sun. I also remember mama sneaking away with Aunt Liz to get my ears pierced. Daddy wanted to wait until I was old enough to make the decision for myself. Mama just wanted me to embrace all things feminine at a young age. All of my lady-like qualities sure come from her. Mama wasn't short-stopping herself. She's known for having the perfect shape. I remember her wearing these yellow shorts (which was a rarity) and the cats in the neighborhood treated her like she was 'Mrs. Parker'. I saw beauty in my parents and that grew within me. It influenced how I physically saw myself and what I wanted to be. I was so glad when mama gave those shorts to me; It's like my fine was activated. This is superhero stuff, you wouldn't understand.

My parents' friends said I was pretty and would grow up to be a model. During that time, I always smiled and loved taking pictures. I was always photo-ready. It only took a moment one day, of kids teasing me about always smiling that diminished it. Shortly after that, I started losing my baby teeth, which was late compared to the other kids that I went to school with. I was still smiling and a teacher (which was not my own) made fun of me in front of my entire class. Totally embarrassed; I began to not feel so comfortable being me. A light in me went out during that very moment.

Afterwards, I was still greatly complimented but, started to hear people tease me about having a big forehead. It is a shame when some black people don't look at "our natural features" as being acceptable or attractive. Later on, a hair stylist told me how beautiful I was; she said she too had a big forehead like mine and believed it should be covered up. I was "too cute" not to look better by doing so, she thought and expressed that to my former beautician. She was a young lady projecting her own insecurities unto a teenage girl. Touching on this, all I can think about is "not the bayang" taking off on social media recently. I have a reoccurring joke as an adult. I often say, "a big head helps you give good head."

I grew up carrying discomfort about my appearance regarding scars and my skin. Dealing with major skin issues, sometimes it became harder to see the beauty within myself. People can be really harsh. When my acne was caked-up on my skin, some of the most destructive comments came from people that loved me. Sometimes I had to look beyond my flaws to see what remained; simply beautiful in my Al Green's voice. It's okay to continuously accept what is and change or improve what you feel can be made to appear better.

I have truly accepted me. I just love me, all of me. I am who I am with no apologies. I have been every size from a 4 to 16. When I was on the thicker side, I referred to myself as a big body Benz. I have flaws and blemishes;

some wrinkles that detail my journey since birth, like lines on the bark of a tree. Moles and beauty marks which I find so cute. I have body freckles all brown but, I especially love my strawberry legs; just planted seeds of goodness. I embrace the yellow girl or redbone in the winter. I also love being 'Caramel Delight' in the summer; as my high school best friend, Marquetia calls me to this day. We have the keys to access our own definition of beauty. Just be comfortable being you. Love you in every form and every stage of life. I am enjoying all of this gorgeous-ness. I look forward to taking better care of "me" and aging gracefully. I even have some grey hairs now. When they first appeared; I was devastated. Then, my friend Magnolia said, "that's your wisdom showing". That gave me warrior-like strength. I plan to be a fine ole' broad in my more mature seasons of life. I appreciate every cute dimple on my body. I know I am getting older so, some of those dimples may turn into dents one day and that is okay. A luxury vehicle can have some knicks but, still look good and ride smooth. Boobs aren't as perky and no longer sit right under my neck. They are still firm and nicely positioned. If gravity ever takes over and they hit the ground, they'll be succulent walking speed bumps to slow me down in life when needed. I am liking my new slimmed down figure. I will love me no matter the size because there will always be something about me worth looking in the mirror at. People keep asking me, "What's your secret?" Well, I have been rocking waist beads and sipping Fannie's CYW pineapple lemonade infused water. I can't give you the entire recipe just yet but, those are some of the ingredients. Let's see how this body turns out before I start giving advice. I appreciate my curves and the way that I carry myself; To my glassy-piercing eyes to my high cheek bones to my plumped lips.

No, it is not all about appearance. Substance and value should be present; along with a good moral compass and a righteous spirit. I am still a firm believer that, when you look good... you feel good. Live and continue to be beautiful Kings and Queens. Keep wearing your crown. I know it gets heavy but, it has been adorned with custom made jewelry just for you. You were born to carry yourself with grace, dignity and confidence.

Chapter Six

Loving Myself Through Thick and Thin

Conchetta Jones

Conchetta Jones is owner of Confident Woman She's All That! coaching, consulting and training company for women. She is a Certified Personal Development and Confidence Coach who motivates and inspires women to step out of their comfort zone and go after the life that they desire and deserve. She is an Author, Model and Speaker. It is the title speaker that she is most proud of, because for years she had a fear of speaking in front of people and failed speech class two times at two different colleges because she could not stand in front of the class to present her speeches. At She's All That! she helps women to identify the obstacles that are keeping them stuck and not allowing them to live the life they want. She shows them how to follow their dreams often using her life experiences as examples.

Conchetta loves working with women and girls. It was her love of working with girls that motivated her to start her non-profit, She's All That! Personal Development and Mentoring Organization. She feels that women are dynamic entities and she loves being in their midst. She especially loves her friendships with younger women. She loves their energy, drive and courage. And feels they help her to stay young.

Conchetta is deeply family-oriented and finds it a blessing to spend time with her family. Her favorite time of year is the Christmas season when she gets to go down south to spend Christmas with her mom. son and grandsons. A leader and influencer in her own right, Conchetta has been in a space of leadership for many years starting as a Sunday School Teacher and Superintendent for over 25 years, to being the current CEO of her own lifestyle coaching company.

Conchetta continues to lead and support women who need guidance as they navigate their life. Now is the perfect time to set goals and plan to reach each one of them. Most of her clients just need to know how to build the path and to choose the direction most suited for them.

conchettajones@gmail.com

www.satwoman.com

Loving Myself Through Thick and Thin

"You're pretty for a brown skin sister"

"Are you Indian?"

"Is that your real hair?"

"That's grandma's black baby"

"Come here black gal"

"You cute, but yo redbone friend over there is prettier"

"I don't think dark skinned sisters are attractive"

These were just some of the things that I heard growing up and also in my adult life. While some were annoying, none of them bothered me as much as the following:

"Hey Olive Oyl"

"Don't nobody want no bone but a dog"

"Skinny Minny"

"Girl you do drugs?"

"My arm is bigger than your leg"

"Can you afford to eat up in Chicago?"

"I seen better legs on a table"

In case you have not caught it yet, my weight was a big problem for me. All of my life I was super skinny. I mean really skinny. It used to bother me; all I wanted was to have big legs. I am from the South, so being skinny was not good at the time. I couldn't be a majorette for my high school because I was too skinny, they wanted the bigger curvier girls to represent the school. Never mind that fact that I could really dance. I just didn't fit the image they wanted. I went through all of the sizes, children's 12-14, adult 0-3; I wore a size 3 for many years and was in my thirties before I moved up to a size 6. When I finally made it to a size 8, I thought I was the stuff, I had hips y'all.

I can remember working in Marshall Fields and every day at lunch time I would stop by this big scale that was outside of the cafeteria. I can remember the day I hit 107 lbs, you would have thought that I had hit the lottery, I had finally made it to the 100-pound club. I know to some people this is nothing, but for me the only time I was 100 plus pounds, was when I was in the labor room about to deliver my son; I weighed 117 pounds that day. However, when they sent me home four days later, I was back down to 95 pounds and a few days after that I was back to my 92-93 pounds. It seemed as if weight just ran away from me. The one good thing that happened to me during my pregnancy was that my breasts went up to a 36C, they stayed that size for about 3 months after childbirth, but after that they went back to my original teeny tiny barely size A cups.

I was really anxious to gain weight. I ate all of the time. I had an appetite like a man twice my size. Even though I ate all of the time, I never gained a pound. I took supplements such as Weight On, drank milk shakes and anything else that was supposed to put meat on these bones. Nothing worked though. My older relatives down south told me that I didn't gain weight because my hair was taking all my nutrients. Y'all know I took their word for gospel and cut my hair. I did not gain a pound. I drank beer, ate so many bananas with peanut butter that it was pathetic…still no weight.

I was often so jealous of my two best friends, Brenda and Melvina, who had big legs and curvy bodies. They looked so good to me in short shorts and Brenda was a majorette. I always felt like some under developed child next to them.

Back in the day, it was not as popular to be skinny as it is today. Having curves was considered desirable. Pam Grier and Thelma from Good Times was the ideal black girl back then. I often struggled with body image issues because of my weight or lack thereof. I was the last girl in my class to wear a bra. Being in the 7th grade and flat chested was not good for my self-esteem. Especially when the boys would go around snapping the girl's bra straps and I had on a tee shirt. When I finally got my first bra, I was so excited. My mom was going to go shopping when she got off work and bring my bra home. I had been hinting around for a bra for a few months. But mom felt I was okay with a tee shirt. So, when she finally agreed that it was time for a bra, I was ecstatic. Finally, I would be wearing a bra like all of the other girls in my class. It was like Christmas Eve that night. She had to work late and then go shopping to get my bra. I finally fell asleep waiting for her, but woke up super early the next day to see my *bra*.

Imagine my disappointment when my "bra" turned out to be a piece of material with straps. No cup at all. I wanted to cry because I could have just kept wearing my tee-shirt. Finally, after a couple of months, I graduated to a bra with a little cup. I was too happy. I was still flat, but I had cups. I started stuffing my bra with socks. Well let me tell you my humiliation when one day I stuffed my bra with red socks. I went to Catholic school and a white blouse was part of the uniform.

During lunch one day we were jumping rope and as I jumped my red socks worked their way up out of the bra and everyone could see. I was mortified, and of course that was the day that the boys were watching. That just gave them more ammunition to tease me with.

When I moved back down south to go to high school, I had a friend who was also a tormentor. He coined the phrase 50 cents worth of neckbones as my nickname. I hated to see him coming because he would yell it down the hallways of our high school. He would make all kinds of fun at my expense. Even though he was a grade ahead of me he was in my math class and instead of doing his work he would be teasing me.

When I got married, my brother-in-law Michael, coined the phrase Skinny-in-law for me. Everyone thought it was funny. Me, not so much. And I was really embarrassed by the name as well as my skinny body. Especially since my two sisters-in-law had curvier bodies.

I soon made peace with my skinny body, flat chest and ability to eat anything I wanted whenever I wanted. I was still envious of the girls with the brick house bodies. And when the Commodores came out with that song "Brick House" I was reminded all over again that I was not a brick house. When we would go out to the club's they would always have a brick house contest and the women with the curvy bodies would head out to the dance floor. I always wanted to join them, but at a size 3, with no chest, I was not hardly a brick house.

Things got a little easier when I moved back to Chicago in the 80's. People were not as fixated on weight as they were down south. And when I started modeling and teaching at Barbizon School of Modeling my weight was a good thing. I can remember smiling smugly when we would go to lunch and the other girls would be counting calories and looking over at my big juicy hamburger, fries and milkshake with envy.

But…once again my skinny body embarrassed me. I started working with Luster Products as one of their production models. What does that mean? It means I traveled with them to the various hair shows and we would put on hair and fashion productions. I loved my job with them. But there was one incident that set the trajectory of my time with them. At one of the first fashion presentations, my flat chest did not fit my costume. The designer, who was a jokester start calling me "Conchester", and teasing me about my raisins. He even rolled up some plastic from a cleaner's bag to stuff my bra with. It didn't help that my little sister, who was also one of the models was very voluptuous and was spilling out of her dress. From that point on, I could not take the stage without my "ta tas". Those were the spongy, lifelike falsies that I purchased from Fredericks of Hollywood. For nine years they were a permanent part of my Model's Bag, and before I took the stage someone would inevitably ask me if I had my ta'tas in. "Yes, I do thank you very much".

I eventually made peace with my skinny body. I started wearing a lot of spandex. Funny, how with spandex on you automatically have a body. I only wore stretch jeans. Anybody remember Jordache`, Calvin Klein and Gloria Vanderbilt? I also gave up wearing bras. Why should I? I did not even fill out an A cup. I still deep down inside craved a bigger, curvier body and was envious of the women who had them. I wanted that so bad. People would always talk about my hair and I would have given that up in a minute for big legs and boobs.

While social media was not as big back then as now, the magazines all screamed how you needed to have curves to be sexy. The rap videos and rappers all rapped about curvy bodies and being a rump shaker. I can remember one day actually crying when I tried on a bra and it actually said 'barely A cup" and it was too big. Talk about messing with my self-esteem.

Then Victoria's Secret came out with the water bra. It pushed you up and out…. and baby I was all for it. With my spandex and my push up bra, honey I was the answer. I loved looking in the mirror.

Well…after many years, I finally started gaining weight in my late 30's. I was a happy girl. As I gained weight, the scale moved and the tape measurements registered a larger number, I was happy. I loved my new body. I had boobs y'all. No more push up bras were necessary. I just felt yummy.

But then with the weight came the restrictions. I could no longer just eat anything anytime. Because now I could gain weight. And too much weight on my short frame comes off dumpy. And then I started feeling some kind of way because I was "fat".

Now when I would go home "down south" people had stuff to say about me being fat. I went home for a funeral and my son's father didn't even recognize me at first. Nobody at home ever expected me to be as big as I was. Even though at my largest I only wore a size 12. Everyone was still amazed.

After many years, I have really come to peace with my body. Whether I have a few extra pounds, or a lack of pounds (has not happened in a few years) I feel pretty good about myself. I no longer let what the media defines as sexy or desirable define me. I know how special my body is. I appreciate what it allows me to do. I appreciate that I am healthy because for many years I suffered with a Thyroid problem that kept me from gaining weight. That was during one of those times when I dropped what little weight (107 pounds) I had gained and went back down to 95 pounds. My clothes hung off of me. People were wondering if I had started doing drugs. But with a hyperactive thyroid I could not keep the weight on. One of the side effects of a hyperactive thyroid is thinning hair. I never had that problem. My hair continued to grow and it was thick. And even if my hair had been thin, I thought that having big legs and boobs were more important than my hair anyway.

That's so funny to me, because my hair has caused girls to want to fight me, have had grown women be mean to me, and all the time I never appreciated it. I was so fixated on what I didn't have. We are often our own worst enemy. While I was dwelling on the fact that I was skinny and not feeling desirable, I never had a problem getting dates. It was my own insecurities that made me feel less than. It was the constant messaging from the media that fed my insecurities. It was the blatant sexuality that was in the magazines that kept them front and center in my mind.

I finally came to terms with my body. And I now have much love for it. It serves me well. Like I tell the girls I mentor and the women I coach; *If it is something that I can change, I will change it. If it is something that I can't I will learn to love it.*

Because I Am More Than JUST My Skin

Chapter Seven

Sometimes You Need an Ally

Latonya Willett

Latonya Brown Willett, a wife of 25 years, mother of 4, financial analyst, entrepreneur, motivational speaker, and Evangelist. Latonya was born on the Westside of Chicago. She's the next to youngest of 4 children. At a very early age, (4 years old) Latonya always had a caring heart for others. She would help others as much as she could by giving of her time, money, toys, and anything else she had to give.

As Latonya became older, she still had a caring spirit, but ran into life along the way. By the age of 15, she had her first child and by the time she was 17 she had her second child. While struggling to keep up her grades and take care of 2 children with the support of only her older sister, her second child would eventually die at the age of 4 months old on Mother's Day from SIDS. Only by the grace of God did Latonya navigate her way through depression, suicide attempts and more, to be able to care for her older son.

4 months after the death of her son, she met the man that would later become her husband. They have 2 sons together and 2 grandsons, one from the oldest and 1 from the middle son.

Latonya has a background in Nursing and Science. Latonya is now and has been a Financial Analyst, for the past 18 years, known as The Money Lady. She analyzes and presents budget plans, investment ideas, as well as provide insurance options. Latonya has won many awards associated with the work she does for her clients, and has been recognized and celebrated as one of the "100 Black Queens of Chicago". She's the Outreach Director of her church as well as an ordained Evangelist, has her own Non-Profit called "Blessings From Heaven". She also helps her 20-year-old son run both of his businesses, Dance Characters and BopKing Larry Entertainment. The 2 of them travel to schools teaching the children about how money works and how they can become business owner's themselves. Latonya is a real Comeback Queen with a demonstrated wealth of knowledge of life's hardships, overcoming obstacles, business, wealth creation, and legacy building.

To contact Latonya Willett, you can reach her by email at LatonyaWillett@yahoo.com

Sometimes You Need an Ally

At an early age, I have always known that I was different. I always felt out of place. In the beginning, I didn't think anything of it. As time went on, I learned some unbelievably valuable lessons about people as well as myself.

It all began when I was 6 years old; At that time, the television show "Fame" was out. I loved to watch Debbie Allen instruct her students on how they were to dance, how they were to hold their posture, as well as how to check their attitudes at the door. I would also watch channel 11, they always had some type of classical dance program on. Watching these shows piqued my interest in wanting to become a ballerina. I would twirl around the house on my tip toes and tell my mother and father that I wanted to be a ballerina. My love for the dance got so intense that I began to beg them. Every day I would ask them about getting me lessons so that I could learn to become a ballerina. They would always say they would check into it, but that would be the end of it. Until, one day, I asked my mother about becoming a ballerina and taking classes, and on this particular day, she laughed at me and said I was too big to be a ballerina. She said I would break my toes because I was too fat. I began to look at myself in the mirror trying to see where I was fat or too big. I wanted to see what she saw. I even asked her, "How am I too big"? She said it was in my butt and that it was too big. From that day forward, I would look in the mirror and compare myself to the adults and pre-teens that I saw on Fame and other shows to see how I was bigger or different than them.

Later, at the age of 7 years old, I would get hit by a car. I stayed in the hospital for several months. I had to have a body cast because my leg and hip was broken. I would often hear my mother tell my aunt and other people that she hoped I would not turn out like a woman she knew that had a limp for the rest of her life. She said the lady was a nice lady, but the only thing "wrong" with her was that she had a limp because one leg was shorter than the other one. When it was time for me to have my cast removed, and go to therapy, I would try to make my leg grow to the length of the other leg. I did this because I did not want to have a limp. I did not want to have anything "wrong" with me.

In school, I never really fit in with the crowd. I tried, but it just did not work. Although, we were on welfare for the most part, the children at school always thought we were rich. They thought that because our apartment was so beautifully decorated, we had expensive and beautiful furniture. Even though, my mother would shop at the thrift stores and good wills for our clothes as well as regular stores, everyone thought we were rich. She never believed in buying name brand clothing, she believed in buying clothing that was timeless, that would never go old and she would wash our best clothes on her hands with

Woolite. So, our clothes looked new for an exceptionally long time. When the children would come to pick me up for school and see our apartment, they would go back to school to tell the others. I went from having no one coming to pick me up, to three and four children coming to pick me up to go to the school. Our school sat right across the vacant lot from my apartment building. It was not long before it went back to being no one coming to pick me up again. The children would begin to call me rich and talk about me. They would say that I thought I was better than them. Which was the furthest thing from the truth. I spent a lot of time trying to fit in and show them that I did not think I was better than them. It did not make matters any better that I had all A's in school. I was then called the nerd or the geek. I could not win for losing.

I was in the "Academic Bowl", which is something like "Know Your Heritage", except we answered questions about all subject matters, like Jeopardy. I recited poems for our school assemblies and for competition's against other schools. I was in countless spelling bees in my school as well as other school's competitions. This is when I found my ally. I came home one day to let my parents know about a poem that I had to have memorized for the school assembly, to my surprise, my father began helping me with my presentation. You must understand, that for the most part, my father was a very silent man that followed my mother's lead on everything. The only time I really heard him voice his opinion on anything was when he would come in late at night drunk and wake my sister up out of her sleep to lecture her. I was her shadow, so I was right there with her for her many nightly lectures. He would always tell her how important she was. He would tell her how valuable she was, and how she should never let herself fall victim to depending on a man for what he can do for her. He always instilled in her that she can do all those things for herself. That she should only have a man or husband out of love and not for finances because of the fear that he would use that against her and mistreat her. I believe he would have these talks with her when he was drunk because of the demons he may have been fighting. He was not a perfect man himself, so I guess he wanted her to have someone better than him.

When he helped me with the poem I had to recite, he told me how my posture should be. He told me to stand up straight, look into the crowd. He taught me how to look above the people's head so that I would not be afraid of their faces. He told me how I should speak loudly and clearly so the people could understand me. He also, told me the night before I was to speak, that I was going to do good and that he was proud of me no matter what happened. Oh my God! That was all the approval I needed. Such a weight had been lifted off my shoulders. It did not matter if I was the rich girl, it did not matter if I was the nerd, or the teacher's pet anymore. At this moment, I was so much more than what everyone else thought of me. All that mattered was I was George Beards' daughter, and he was going to love me even if I messed up.

Parent's, teacher's, and people in general, I think, miss out on this small principle. They are so busy putting the pressure on their children, friends, and family of being perfect that they forget to convey the fact that, they will still love them, even if they fail. This brings so much pressure and anxiety to people to be perfect that some people never even start. When my father conveyed his love for me, this made me think back to when my parents would have parties. They would invite all their friends over and I would be the entertainment. We had a "hi-fi" (record player) that could take the music out of a song or take the words out of a song and only play the music. My parents would take the singing out of the song and let the music play so that I could sing the song on top of the music. I had an exceptionally good voice at an early age. Their friends loved it. I could remember that when I was done entertaining, my father would introduce me to his friends as his baby. He would say that I was his heart and the sun rose and set on me. I was so young, I never understood what he meant. I would ask everyone where their heart was. I would think, if the heart is in your chest, how can I be his heart, is his heart not still in his chest? I would go outside to see if the sun were shining. I would walk around, and it seemed as if the sun was following me. I would look at my butt to see if the sun was coming out of it, or if it was going in when the sun was setting. I was a little 5 and 6-year-old girl. I took everything literally at that time. I did not understand figurative language back then.

I tried everything I could to fit in. I threw myself into everything, not only because I had an interest in it, but also because I wanted to occupy myself so that I would not care about how I wasn't able to fit in. I later became a cheerleader. I even tried out for the basketball team, but I didn't make the cut. I tutored the children in the lower grades and some in my class. I even tutored a girl that was my bully. I've always had a heart to forgive and help others, no matter how bad they've been to me. I believe that's why I was always rejected from all the people I tried to fit in with. I believe it was all in God's plan to keep me from the dangers, seen and unseen. He really does take care of babies and fools. I think I was a little bit of both. I was able to see that the same people that I was trying to fit in with, would always end up in trouble. Either trouble with the teachers, the law, drugs, or death.

Even as I got older, I still did not fit in with most people. When I started to come into my body, my mother would shame me and say that I wanted to be grown because I looked grown. She would say that I must think I'm something just because my body looked a certain way. So, I would try to downplay my body and the way I walked so I would not seem as if I was trying to be sexy. When I started college, she began to tell me to not forget where I came from and that I was still not anybody special just because I was going to school.

I have never been the type of person that could intentionally do harm to a person. I could not be the type of person that could make fun of a person's downfall. So, for that reason, I was still rejected by grown people whom you'd think would know better than to act this way. You must also understand that these grown-ups are just grown bodied children who never really grew up past what they were taught or what was done to them. Now, they carry it over into adulthood and continue the cycle with their children. Even the ones in the church. That is a story for another time.

John 15:19 *If ye were of the world, the world would love his own: but because ye are not of the world, but I have chosen you out of the world, therefore the world heateth you.*

Romans 12:2 *And be not conformed to this world: but be ye transformed by the renewing of your mind, that ye may prove what is good, and acceptable, and perfect, will of God.*

There came a time when I had to stop looking at everyone else and what they wanted me to be and look at myself. I had to do a self-check to see what I was really doing. Was I hurting anyone, was I rude to anyone, was I trying to hurt anyone? The answer to all those questions were "No". Was I trying to help people, was I trying to be there for people, was I trying to make a difference in my life, my family's life, and the lives of others? The answers to all those questions was "Yes". So, I had to just stop caring about what others thought of me. In the words of Mary J. Blige, I was just fine!

I look back on all those times I tried to fit in, or I tried to be perfect to please people, and I also think about my father. I think about the love he had for me. I think about the words he would say to my sister and me. I think about the way he made me feel through his words and his loving touch and it just makes things so much better. They say you marry your father, so when I long for the love of my father, I can always go to my husband for encouraging words. But, when my husband is at work and I need someone, I can always count on Jesus. He is always there.

Psalm 121:1,2 *I will lift up mine eyes unto the hills, from whence cometh my help. My help cometh from the Lord, which made heaven and earth.*

Psalm 46:1 *God is our refuge and strength, a very present help in trouble.*

Matthew 28:20 *Teaching them to observe all things whatsoever I have commanded you: and, lo, I am with you always, even unto the end of the world. Amen.*

Psalm 139:14 *I will praise thee; for I am fearfully and wonderfully made: marvellous are thy works; and that my soul knoweth right well.*

For years, I have always wanted to fit in and be

accepted by others. That is, until I saw what fitting in can do to you. I saw that it can be detrimental to you and your health, and some people were just not worth my time or presence. Once, I saw the beauty of and in me, and I embraced every part of me, I saw that I was meant to stand out. I am marvelously and wonderfully made. Now, I can freely and unapologetically live in my freedom and purpose. This is why, I am more than just the skin I'm in!

Because I Am More Than JUST My Skin

Conclusion

Thank you for taking the time to read "Because I Am More Than JUST My Skin"

In this anthology, we the Authors, wanted to share our story of learning, loving and becoming of ourselves with you the readers. We wanted you to know that we too have had some "skin" mountains to climb and get over. We want you to remember that you can and will get through this.

The bible says **Psalm 139:13–14** *For you created my inmost being; you knit me together in my mother's womb. I praise you because I am fearfully and wonderfully made; your works are wonderful, I know that full well.* This scripture tells us that we are wonderful no matter what "they" think we look like!

Also remember that God hears all of your silent hurts, He sees your tears and He made you on purpose for purpose. You have to continue to work on you, continue to heal yourself, continue to have faith in knowing God loves you Because You Are More Than JUST Your Skin…

Thank you!

Because I Am More Than JUST My Skin